THE FIRST BOOK of

FESTIVALS

AROUND THE WORLD

FRANKLIN WATTS
NEW YORK

ALMA KEHOE RECK   pictures by HELEN BORTEN

Copyright ©1957 by Franklin Watts, Inc.
Printed in the United States of America
by the Polygraphic Company of America, Inc.
Published in Canada by Ambassador Books, Ltd., Toronto 1, Ontario
First printing
Library of Congress Catalog Card Number: 57-7539

The author's and publishers' thanks to *Children's Activities*
for permission to include *The Befana Fair, The Candy Festival,* and *The Pony-penning,* first published in that magazine.

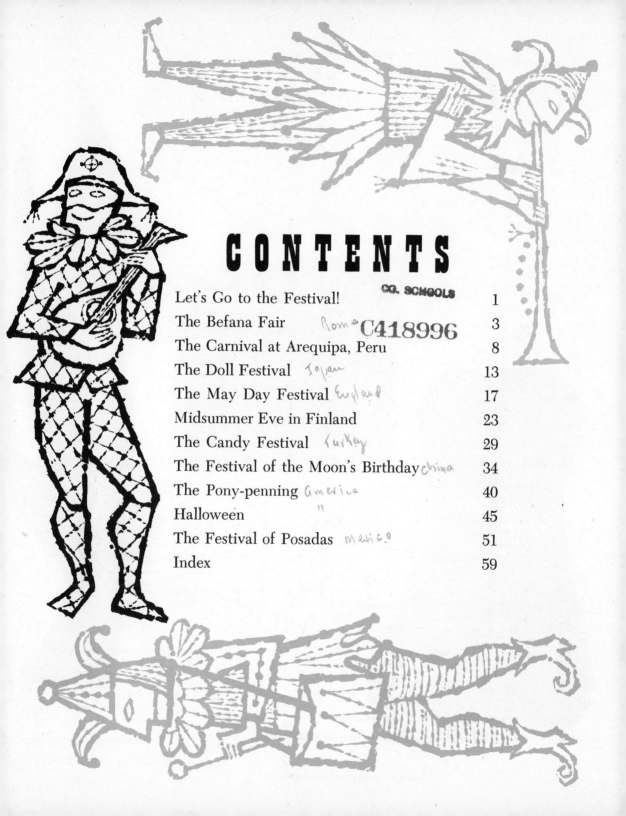

CONTENTS

Let's Go to the Festival!

A festival is a celebration — a time of fun and merry-making. It can celebrate almost anything: seeding time or harvest time, a change in the seasons, a religious holiday, the homecoming of an important person, or a great victory. A festival is a wonderful way to express joy and give thanks for something that has happened.

The word festival comes from the Latin word *festum*, which means "holiday" or "feast," and feasts and festivals are as old as time. In early days the people found planting in the spring and harvest in the fall times for great rejoicing. They celebrated the coming of the new moon and the full moon because the moon took away darkness. The ancient Greeks and Romans had many celebrations. With the coming of Christ the Christians took over many of the old festivals and gave them a Christian meaning.

Every nation has special festivals, and each festival has special customs. At some, people celebrate with athletic games and folk dances. At others they build bonfires and set off fireworks. At many they give presents to one another. But whatever they do, it is because their hearts are filled with happiness. Festivals everywhere are joyous times.

Let's go to the festival!

The Befana Fair

"Che gioia! What fun!" black-eyed Beppo shouts, and blows his whistle into his sister Maria's ear. And for once no one says "Be quiet!" for all the family is making as much noise as Beppo.

They are having a gay time at the famous Befana Fair. It comes each year on January 5, the eve of Epiphany, which celebrates the coming of the Three Kings with gifts for the Christ Child in Bethlehem. The fair is held in Rome, Italy, in the Piazza Navona. The Piazza is a great open square where, almost two thousand years ago, the Emperor Domitian raced his horses.

On this evening the square is a happy place, bright with hundreds of twinkling lights. They shine on many-colored booths where there are toys of all kinds to delight Italian boys and girls. Dolls, toy carts and trains, jumping jacks, music boxes, balls, kites, sailboats, tiny tea sets, and many other toys are there.

As the children enter the square they are given tin trumpets or whistles in the shape of a little old woman with a broom and a basket. She is called Befana, and it is for her the fair is named.

As the evening grows darker, hundreds of people — boys and girls, mothers and fathers, uncles and aunts and grandparents — crowd into the square. They walk about, greet-

3

ing one another, buying sweets, and looking at the toys. And each person tries to see who can make the most noise with his Befana whistle. Shouts of laughter go up as groups of friends meet one another with a deafening din.

Trumpeters march around the Piazza, and bands of music-makers add their share to the noise. It becomes louder. But the people in the booths do not mind.

"It is an old custom," they say. "The greater the noise, the better the Befana Fair!"

And who is this Befana for whom the fair is named? The legend goes that over 1,900 years ago a little old woman named Befana lived in a cottage beside a road where caravans of camels passed.

On the eve of January 6, Befana was busy with her household duties when three strange men came to her door. They were dressed in rich robes and spoke in an unknown language, but she understood one to say his name was Gaspar. The second, a long-haired, gray-bearded old man, said his name was Melchior. The third man, Balthasar, had dark skin and a bushy black beard. The three men told of following a bright star, and they asked the way to Bethlehem. They invited the old woman to go with them.

But Befana only thumped her broom and answered gruffly, "Can't you see that I am busy sweeping?"

"Do come with us to see the *Gesu Bambino*, the Infant Jesus," Gaspar said.

4

"We are taking gifts to Him," Melchior added.

"Surely you have some little gift for Him," Balthasar suggested.

But Befana only thumped her broom again.

"When I finish sweeping, I must bring in the wood," she said.

5

A little later a shepherd boy came to her door.

"Come to Bethlehem with me," he said. "We will find the Holy Babe and Mary and Joseph."

Again Befana shook her head.

"I must cook the supper now. Perhaps in the morning I will go."

Late that night Befana looked out her window. She saw the sky trembling with light and filled with angels. Then she knew something very important had happened at Bethlehem.

She decided to go at once. She packed in her basket the few toys she could find around the house, and she blew out the candle and locked the door. But she soon learned that she could not find the way in the dark. And in the morning no one on the road seemed to know how to get to Bethlehem. Up and down the roads she went, over the fields and through the woods, saying over and over, "I must find the Christ Child!"

But she never found Him.

The legend is that from that day to this she has traveled everywhere, searching in vain. On the eve of Epiphany, the night the Three Kings journeyed to Bethlehem, Befana with her broom and her basket of toys is said to go from house to house in Italy. She looks into the faces of the sleeping children and asks, "Is He here? Is the Christ Child here?"

Before she leaves the bedroom she takes toys and candies from her basket and leaves them for the sleeping child. She puts them on the pillow, in his pocket, or in his stocking. If the child has been naughty during the year she leaves only a bit of charcoal.

So every year on this evening, not only in Rome but in many other Italian cities, people of all ages hold festivals where they make a great noise in Befana's honor, just as Beppo and Maria are doing.

But now it is nearly midnight at Rome's Befana Fair. The noise is dying down and Beppo and Maria are growing tired.

"Come, we will go now," their mother says.

Once at home, they fall into bed to dream of the festival — all the toys they have seen, the noise they have made, the sweets they have eaten, the fun they have had.

When morning comes a few hours later, they jump out of bed to see if Befana has paid them a visit.

"*Ecco la Befana!* Look, Befana!" the children shout when they find the gifts she has left for them.

The Carnival at Arequipa, Peru

"What color does this make?"

Little Esteban runs the dark powder through his fingers, and his black eyes light up with interest. He and his sister Rosita are visiting the big central market at Arequipa, Peru, where they find powders of many colors on display in open barrels.

The merchant looks closely at the dark powder, stops to study a label, and says, "This is green."

Esteban giggles as he says, "I'll buy some of this green, and some red, and some blue, and some yellow!"

A tourist from the United States who stands nearby is curious. "What is this powder?" he asks. "And what are the children going to do with it?"

The merchant tries to hold back a smile. "Just wait until carnival time," he says, "and *you'll find out!*"

Before the children leave the market they stop to admire the baskets filled with masks, false noses, paper hats, and balloons — all of which they will see at the carnival. Another basket holds *serpentina,* long paper streamers in a rainbow of colors.

8

"Now let's go home and make *cascarones*," Rosita suggests, and Esteban agrees.

To make *cascarones*, Rosita and Esteban will open eggs at one end and empty from them the yolk and white. Then the children will fill the eggshells with many-colored confetti, and seal them shut with a bit of gummed tape.

The carnival takes place a day or so before the beginning of Lent, usually about the middle of February. Because Peru is south of the equator, January, February, and March are summer months. This means vacation time for school children, so everyone has plenty of time to get ready for the festival.

Arequipa is one of the largest cities in Peru, South America. About 120,000 people live there. Many of Arequipa's buildings are white, and the fields around the city are so green that people often describe it as a "diamond surrounded by emeralds." It curls at the foot of the volcano El Misti, which is over 19,000 feet high, but is no longer active.

At carnival time there is usually a parade of floats, gay with beautiful decorations. Everyone admires them, saying "Oh!" and "Ah!" as they pass along the streets. Many of the people along the way wear costumes. Angels and devils, lords and ladies, princes and princesses, clowns, birds, and animals dance along to the lilting music of the bands.

9

But it is after the parade that the real fun begins on the streets that lead to the Plaza de Armas. This is a palm-shaded little park in the center of the city.

Then hundreds of young boys appear. They carry baskets of *cascarones*, and these are filled, not with confetti, but with *water*, colored and very wet! Yes, this is what the dye is used for.

Two boys come out on the balcony of a house across the

plaza. Plop! a *cascarón* breaks on one of the boys' heads, and the boy is colored a beautiful blue! The other boy is soon splashed with pink water.

But the two boys on the balcony have ammunition, too. A paper bag filled with colored water is tossed below to douse the *cascarón* throwers in a golden shower. A balloon filled with crimson water lands with a beautiful *bloop* and changes the gold to a bright orange.

11

The water fight is on — the most brilliant water fight ever — and everyone has a wonderful time. Not only boys and girls, but men and women join in the fun. Buckets and basins, each holding a different color, are made ready on the balconies.

People down on the street prepare for the water battle, too. A group of youths in a truck drive into the plaza. In the back of the truck there is a five-gallon can of water, colored a rich purple. The youths use a pump to spray those on the balcony with the royal shade.

The people on the balcony empty their buckets and pans, and soon the youths below look like Easter eggs. But the people above haven't finished. They dump a basket of confetti over the boys below, who now look as if they had a case of many-colored measles!

At sundown the men and women go home to dress for the dances that are held during the evening.

Estaban and Rosita, looking like rainbows, admire their reflections in the mirror at home. Their mother tells them to wash off the harmless vegetable dyes in a warm bath, but they do not want to.

"But Mamacita, I look so gay this way!" Rosita says. "Let me look bright a little longer!"

"Carnival time is such fun," Estaban agrees, "and it will be a whole year before it comes again! Please let us make it last a few hours more!"

The Doll Festival

"Please do come in!" Kimiko bows low as she greets her little friend Fumiko at the door. Kimiko wears her very best silk kimono of deep rose and violet brocade. Her *obi*, or wide sash, is of turquoise blue and gold.

Fumiko wears her best kimono, too. She looks like a big butterfly in apple-green silk, brocaded in white. Her *obi* is made of rose and silver silk.

Today is March 3, the day of the Girls' Doll Festival, and all over Japan little girls play hostess to their friends and are honored by their families.

The dolls that have the central places in this festival are not those that the children play with. Instead, they are ancestral dolls that have been handed down from parents to children over many, many years. Each year the dolls are shown in the same way, according to rules laid down long, long ago.

13

A stand of five or seven shelves is covered with a red cloth, because red is the color of peach blossoms, the rising sun, and happiness.

On the top shelf the Emperor and Empress dolls are placed. Kimiko's Emperor doll is dressed in white satin, with a coat of gold and black brocade. On his head he wears a black crown.

The Empress doll is dressed with great richness. Her crown of shining gold and sparkling jewels towers high above her head. In her tiny hand she holds a fan with ribbon streamers of violet, gold, blue, jade green, and rose.

At either side of the royal pair there are dainty Japanese lanterns which cast a cheery glow over the scene. On the shelf below them are the three ladies-in-waiting of the court. They wear kimonos of white silk, and red pleated skirts fall softly about their tiny feet.

On the next shelf come the five court musicians, dressed in green. Each holds a different musical instrument with which to entertain the royal court.

Below the musicians stand two imperial guardsmen, carrying long bows and arrows. Beside them are three court attendants, holding the Emperor's umbrella, shoes, and hat. On either side of them there are usually tiny orange or cherry trees, sometimes in full bloom.

Somewhere on the stand there will be an elderly couple — Joe San with a rake, and Uba San with a broom. The pair are said to have worked at the royal palace long ago. They found great happiness in their work.

On the bottom shelf tiny pieces of furniture are arranged: small kimono racks, little trays and dishes of lacquer ware, beautiful little vases, and other articles needed for royal housekeeping. And on the little dishes a feast is spread.

Around the stand there is a group of other dolls. These are the ones that the children play with, and sometimes there are a hundred of them. When a baby girl is born in Japan, friends and relatives send dolls as gifts. On the day of the Doll Festival each girl is given more dolls, and she will keep all of them with loving care through the years. When a Japanese girl marries she takes her doll collection with her to her new home.

The young daughter of the family usually plans and

cooks the food that is served the visitors on this day. The little girl prepares a large quantity of rice cake in three layers — red, white, and green — and cuts it into pretty diamond shapes for serving. She also prepares popped beans, popped rice, sugar cookies, and perhaps a bit of white *sake*, a drink made from rice.

Before Kimiko serves her guests she first bows low to the imperial pair on the stand, and offers them a bit of food.

The Doll Festival is a day of great joy and happiness for everyone. The girls like the importance of being hostess, and they enjoy the gay parties and the visiting back and forth. The boys like the good food that is served, and the excitement of the day. The festival is a favorite with parents because it helps them show their love for their daughters.

In Japan the Girls' Doll Festival is sometimes called the Peach Blossom Festival, for it usually comes when the peach trees are blooming. The light pink of the blossoms seems to express the gentle sweetness of the Japanese girls.

Fumiko admires Kimiko's dolls and enjoys the delicious food she is served. Finally it is time to go. Fumiko bows low as she takes leave of her friend Kimiko.

"I've enjoyed seeing your display of dolls," she says. "Now won't you come see mine? I know you like the Girls' Doll Festival as much as I do."

The May Day Festival

"Oh, I feel so happy and gay. Tomorrow I'll be Queen of the May!" Margaret sings, as she and her brother Dick stand watching their mother prepare the flower garlands and staves that will be needed for the May Day Festival.

It is April 30, the day before May Day, in Barrington on the river Cam in England. Barrington is a pretty little village built around a seven-acre green where the festival will be held on the morrow, to celebrate the return of spring.

Long before May Day everybody begins to prepare for it. The teachers must choose dances, and the children must learn them. The boys and girls must also vote for the new May Queen, and she must make ready her royal robes.

A day or two before the great day the children wander over the countryside, looking for wild flowers. And they beg garden blossoms from neighbors and friends. They need the flowers to make garlands for the girls and staves for the boys. The mothers start this work. Grandmothers often help, for making the garlands and staves is an art handed down from parent to child over hundreds of years.

17

First the workers bunch the flowers into little nosegays, then they tie them to moss-covered willow boughs for making garlands, and to narrow strips of wood for making staves.

May Day dawns bright and clear. The Maypole is set up in the center of the green. The guests arrive, and the Three Processions begin. The day is warm with sunshine, and the crowd is gay as the First Procession enters. It is that of the Forget-me-not Queen, the May Queen of the year before, with her royal attendants. They circle the green in a solemn line, and the Queen takes her place on the throne.

Then comes the Procession of the Children. It makes a pretty picture with the girls in bright dresses, bearing their garlands in graceful arches above their heads. Each boy is dressed in his very best, and he carries his flowery stave before him.

Two by two the children curtsy before the Forget-me-not Queen, and take their places on either side of her throne.

A great shout goes up as Margaret, the new May Queen, enters. She is followed by an attendant carrying her scepter, and a page boy bearing her crown on a silk-covered cushion. They are in the Third Procession.

The two queens greet each other, and the new May Queen takes the former queen's place on the throne. Margaret's blue eyes dance with delight as the Forget-me-not

Queen places the crown on her golden curls and says, "I crown you Queen of the May!"

All the children return to honor the new May Queen with a salute or curtsy.

Then the queen commands the festival to go on. First comes the judging of staves and garlands. Boys and girls walk round and round before the judges. One by one the pretty flower pieces are voted out of the race until only three boys and three girls are left with theirs.

Dick is one of the boys, and Margaret, the May Queen, can hardly hold back her cry of pleasure when the judge at last announces, "Dick wins first prize for the prettiest stave."

Next comes the old-time garland dance performed each year by the girls. Each little girl holds her sweet-smelling garland high with pride as her feet twinkle in and out in the pattern of the dance. A stave dance for the boys follows, and they do it perfectly. Not a boy misses a step.

Now come the time-honored dances around the Maypole in the center of the green. One of the best-liked is the Spider's Web. At the end of this dance one of the boys, pretending to be the spider, climbs to the very top of the Maypole, where he is cheered by all for his agility and speed.

The very small children of Barrington are dressed in brilliant red uniforms, and wear caps of yellow. They form

20

a percussion band which supplies music for the festival — and many laughs to the guests.

The last sight of the day is a masque, or play, handed down from the days of Queen Elizabeth I. The boys and girls stand still to represent trees and flowers, while ballet dancers swirl around them.

The festival ends with the handing out of prizes and refreshments for all, from queen to commoner.

"Wasn't it a wonderful day?" Margaret asks Dick, as the festival ends and they cross the green to the little thatched cottage where they live. "And next year will be fun, too," she adds, "for next year I'll be the Forget-me-not Queen!"

Midsummer Eve in Finland

"Hjalmar, come help me put this birch bough over the mirror!" Marta calls from inside the house. "It's so high I can't reach."

"I'm sorry, Marta," her brother calls back, "but I'm working on the birch arch in front of the door. I must get it finished before train time. Can't you use the stepladder?"

It is the morning of June 23, and all over Finland people are getting ready for the Festival of Midsummer Eve. This is the time when the sun reaches the highest point in the sky, and the people take joy in the long days of sunshine after their winter of twilight.

Just as the fir tree is the expression of Christmas time, so the white-barked birch with its slender branches and soft green leaves is the sign of the midsummer festivals in the Scandinavian countries. Pictures, windows, and doorways are framed with the graceful birch boughs. An archway of birch adds its beauty to every house in the village. Avenues of birch lead from houses to barns. In the forests boys and girls dance around the birch trees.

Nowhere in Finland do people celebrate Midsummer Eve with more delight than in Rovaniemi, the little trading town where Marta and Hjalmar live. This village is only a few miles south of the Arctic Circle. There the sun shines for the full twenty-four hours on Midsummer Day. That is why visitors come from all over Finland, Norway, and Sweden to make merry on the holiday.

Marta and Hjalmar finish their decorating in time to go to the station at noon to meet the train from the south. Even the big locomotive wears garlands of birch branches as it puffs to a stop.

"There are Tante Greta and Uncle Nils . . . and Sig and Ingrid!" Marta cries, and rushes to greet them.

The children's visitors live on a small farm in Sweden, so first of all they want to visit the market place. They find it lively indeed, with hundreds of people wandering about, greeting and gossiping, buying and selling.

The women and girls wear brightly striped skirts, tight-laced bodices, and brilliant caps or headbands.

The Laplanders add color, too, in their blue felt tunics, trimmed with red and yellow bands.

"Oh, look at the big copper cooking pots!" Tante Greta exclaims, while Uncle Nils goes to see the large displays of furs and skins. He sees skins of deer, fox, wolf, ermine, bear and rabbit.

Sig chooses a new pair of brown boots, and Ingrid buys an embroidered apron.

During the warm afternoon there is an athletic meet on the meadow. The villagers and their guests are filled with the holiday spirit. They run foot races, throw the hammer and discus, and vault with poles.

After the meet is over and the prizes have been given out, everyone sits on the grass for a picnic supper of salmon, water rolls, fancy cakes, and coffee. Then they all sing the old songs of Finland — songs about the rivers and lakes, the forests and the people. Uncle Nils knows all the words.

When the singing is over, the villagers and their guests scatter to the forest in search of dry wood. This will be burned in *kokkos,* giant bonfires lighted on the stroke of midnight. In the olden days many people believed that these bonfires kept away evil spirits. Today they are looked on as a sign of warmth and light because they overcome cold and darkness.

After the wood is collected, the Maypole, circled with birch boughs and trimmed with wreaths and garlands, is raised and all the people begin to dance around it. They dance with happiness because the winter is over and the summer is theirs to enjoy.

The men and boys dance with their arms folded across their chests, and the women put their hands on their hips. Every dance tells a story, such as one of sowing and reaping, or courting and quarreling. Many people who have not danced all year dance around the Maypole on Midsummer Eve.

"Watch Tante Greta and Uncle Nils . . . they're good!" Hjalmar whispers to Marta, as they pass in the double cir-

25

cle weaving in and out around the Maypole. And it is true.
Tante Greta and Uncle Nils know the old dances perfectly.

As the hour of midnight draws near, the gay dancing
ceases. All the dancers gather in silence around the piles of
wood. They look at the sun still high in the sky, and they
talk in whispers as the clock strikes twelve. The bonfires
are lighted. Finland's flag of white and blue is first dipped,
then raised to the top of the Maypole. Guns are fired, and

26

a great cheer goes up. Then the merrymakers bow their heads and sing the national anthem of Finland, "Thou Land, Our Land, Our Fatherland."

The fires burn lower and lower. They are almost out. Then Marta and Hjalmar, all the other villagers, and their guests prepare to go home.

Hjalmar yawns as he says, "Well, Midsummer Eve is over for another year."

"Yes," Marta agrees, "but it is still *midsummer*. We shall have many more weeks to enjoy the sunshine!"

27

The Candy Festival

"Ahmed, we're going to buy the candy for the Candy Festival," Selika calls to her brother. "Hurry, if you want to go with us."

Ahmed comes hurrying into the room, saying, "Of course I want to go. Is Belkis coming, too?"

"Yes. You know she likes to help choose the different kinds of candy, even if she is only four. And it takes lots of candy for everyone to eat all he wants for three whole days!"

American mothers would say, "Too much candy spoils your dinner." American dentists would say, "Too much candy ruins the teeth." But in faraway Turkey across the sea, Sheker Bairām, or the Candy Festival, is one of the gayest holidays of all the year. Everyone enjoys it, especially because it comes right after Ramadan, a religious fasting period of the Turkish people.

29

The fun really begins a few days before the holiday, when parents and children go from candy shop to candy shop to choose the sweets from big glass jars.

Once the children are at their favorite shop Selika points to several jars which contain hard candies. As the candy man removes the lids a delightful fragrance fills the air, for the candies are flavored with strawberry and rose, orange and lemon, cinnamon, coffee, and bergamot.

"We'll want plenty of Jordan almonds," Ahmed suggests, "and hazel and pistachio nuts, too."

Little Belkis especially likes the *loukam*, or Turkish delight, which another clerk is slicing from big bright sheets on the counter. *Loukam* is made with gelatine, so that it is chewy like gumdrops or marshmallows. It is colored ruby red or emerald green and is rolled in powdered sugar.

As the candy boxes rise higher and higher on the counter, friends and relatives come into the shop. As each one leaves, he says, "Be sure to come see us during Sheker Bairām!" For this is a great time for paying calls. Young people call on their parents the first day. Parents visit their married children in their homes on the second day. And friends pay social calls on the third day.

When they have settled the candy problem, the children go in search of handkerchiefs. For during Sheker Bairām it is also the custom to give these bright squares to friends, relatives, neighbors, and those who serve.

30

When they are home again, Ahmed and Selika wrap the handkerchiefs in gay colored paper. In some of them they tie a coin for an extra-special gift.

Next, the candy tray is made ready with three of the nicest glass bowls from the cupboard. One bowl holds the hard candies, another holds the *loukam,* and a third the nuts. Several glasses for water are also placed on the tray.

The children wake up early on the first morning of Sheker Bairām. Selika and Belkis put on their best silk dresses.

Selika's dress is rose and blue, and Belkis wears a frock of violet. They tie white silk squares on their heads. Ahmed wears his best clothes, too.

All three are eager to see who will be the first visitor, and soon little Belkis shouts, "Here comes the night watchman."

The watchman makes a gay sight as he rides along on his bicycle, for he carries a long pole hung with dozens of bright-colored handkerchiefs already given him by his friends along the street. He greets the children with a cheery "Happy Bairām to you all!" then helps himself to the candy and water. The children give him a brightly wrapped handkerchief.

After the night watchman come the milkman, the bread man, the vegetable man, the newsboy, and several others. All of them enjoy the candy and gifts which the children have to offer.

During the afternoon Ahmed, Selika, and Belkis go with their parents to visit their grandparents.

"A happy Bairām to you!" they all say together, and they kiss the hands of their elders, then help themselves from the candy tray.

On the way home they stop at an empty lot where a merry-go-round has been set up for the holiday.

"*Lemon su! Lemon su!*" a street seller shouts, and the children have a glass of lemonade — and more candy.

Nearby a stand has been set up for the Karageuz show. Karageuz is a jester or clown who is the leading character in all Turkey's Karageuz plays. These are puppet plays, given somewhat as Punch and Judy shows are, except that the characters are not rounded, but flat like pieces of cardboard. They throw shadows on a white screen behind which there is a brilliant light. Little Belkis claps her hands with delight at their tricks.

The second and third days of Sheker Bairām are much like the first, with plenty of candy, of course, and dancing, races, and wrestling matches. The children display their handkerchief gifts wherever they go.

By nightfall on the third day most of the candy is gone. The parents are tired, and the children are even more weary.

"I don't believe I want any more candy for a while," Selika says, as she gets ready for bed.

Then they all go to sleep beneath the slender crescent moon. Sheker Bairām, the Candy Festival, is over for another year.

The Festival of the Moon's Birthday

"Honorable Grandfather, are you planning to buy a moon rabbit for me?" Kwang Ling tugs at his grandfather's blue cotton gown. He gazes with longing at the little red and green painted clay figures in the market place.

"They look so much like the rabbit one sees on the moon. And I would so like to have one for the Festival of the Moon's Birthday."

Kwang Ling's old grandfather smiles. "Yes, you may have one," he says. "And we must pick out a new doll for your sister, Mei Chu. And what shall we choose for Younger Brother?"

34

Kwang Ling's dark eyes light up. He has a wonderful idea. "Let's buy a pet for him! Let's buy a singing cricket in a little bamboo cage!"

It is the Fifteenth Day of the Eighth Moon, according to the Chinese Year, and all over China people celebrate the Birthday of the Moon. It is a happy holiday — the night of all the year when the moon is at its clearest and brightest, and perfectly round. The holiday comes at harvest time, when the people are glad because of the good summer crops that will supply them with food through the winter.

On a table in the courtyard each family displays the fruits of the harvest, especially those that are round. Among them are bright yellow mandarin oranges from the south and big red persimmons from the north. There are also a few sheaves of grain and two bean stalks with leaves for the moon rabbit.

Best of all the children like the moon cakes, baked especially for the festival. They are made of pale yellow flour and brown sugar, and are stuffed with sweetened soy beans and shelled melon seeds, mixed with egg yolks. The cakes are round like the moon. On top of them there are gay decorations of moon rabbits, crescents, and tiny pagodas in red, yellow, and green.

During the day the streets of the villages are merry. There is music everywhere. People carry baskets covered

with red paper and filled with ham, moon cakes, and other gifts for friends and relatives. As the people walk along, they pause now and then to watch the gay tricks of the lion dancers and the stilt walkers. The boys and girls wear strange masks, to add to the fun.

During the evening, Kwang Ling's family and its friends gather in the moonlight of the courtyard. The place has a holiday look, with chrysanthemums flowering in pots in the corners, red candles burning, and the sweet smell of incense filling the air. Behind the festival table is a paper scroll with a picture of the moon rabbit sitting under the Sacred Cinnamon Tree. Bright strings of paper money hang here and there.

The children feel important, dressed in their very best clothing. They enjoy themselves in trying to see pictures in the moon's face.

"Yes, now I see the moon rabbit!" Kwang Ling exclaims. "He looks just like my little statue. He is standing on his hind legs and stirring something in a bowl with his stick."

Honorable Grandfather pats the boy on the shoulder. "The moon rabbit mixes powders and pills that will make men live forever," he says.

Exactly at midnight firecrackers are set off with a merry pop. Then everyone is ready to eat the festival meal of pork and chicken, bamboo shoots and rice, spicy moon cakes and tea, followed by delicious pieces of brown taffy.

"Honorable Grandfather, please tell us the legend of the Birthday of the Moon," Mei Chu begs.

The old man strokes his wispy gray beard and begins, "Many, many years ago when the world was young, the Emperor Ming Wong walked in his garden with his friend, a priest. The Emperor looked at the moon and found its beauty a delight. He said, 'I wonder what it is like on the moon.'

"Then the priest said, 'Let us go see.'

"He held out his staff, and at once it became a magic bridge. They walked across it to the moon.

"They found the moon a wonderful land indeed, bright with shining white palaces, many-colored pagodas, and snow-white flowers.

"The Emperor picked a bouquet of the flowers before he departed. As the two men walked slowly back to earth along the magic bridge, the Emperor played on his lute. The lovely melody drifted down to the earth, and all over China people ran out to listen and wonder. Then the Emperor tossed the white blossoms from his bouquet and gold coins from his pockets down to the earth below.

"Several days after he was back on earth the Emperor received letters asking the reason for these strange happenings. Then he sent out a proclamation: This night of marvels occurred because it was the moon's birthday. Hereafter it shall be celebrated on the Fifteenth Day of the

Eighth Moon all over the land!"

The children are delighted with the story, and clap their hands.

Then Honorable Grandfather says, "It is time for boys and girls to go to bed. But first let us burn the scroll with the picture of the moon rabbit."

As the flames destroy the scroll, Honorable Grandfather says, "Now the moon rabbit will return to the moon."

The children rise and say, "Thank you for the presents, Honorable Grandfather."

Then they bow low in the direction of the moon.

"Happy birthday! Happy birthday!" they shout. And the Birthday of the Moon Festival is over.

The Pony-penning

"What am I bid for this fine pony?" The auctioneer raps his gavel on the auction block and goes on before anyone has time to answer. "He's sturdy, strong, and friendly . . . a wonderful saddle pony for your children! Now, how much am I bid? Two hundred dollars. . . . Who'll make it two hundred?"

"Bid, Dad, bid! He's the one I want!" Billy begs his father. His blue eyes shine with excitement.

Billy's younger sister Betty likes the pony too. "Oh, Daddy, I think he's beautiful!" she cries, jumping up and down on her toes.

The auctioneer notices the pony's rough brown coat. "Well, he looks a little shaggy now, but a few buckets of oats and a currycomb will make him a beauty in no time! Now, how much am I bid?"

It is the last Thursday in July — Pony-penning Day on Chincoteague Island, off the coast of Virginia. The island wears a holiday air, for this is the high point of a yearly celebration put on by the island's volunteer fire department.

It is round-up day for the wild ponies that roam the pastures of Chincoteague, Assateague, and Wallop's Islands. Some of the animals are branded and left on the islands. Others are sold at auction. On Pony-penning Day people from all over the country come here to choose ponies for their children.

Chincoteague is a pretty island about nine miles long and a mile and one-half wide. About four thousand people live on the island in pretty houses painted white, pink, tan, blue, red, or yellow. Handsome pine, myrtle, and magnolia trees shelter the houses, and mocking birds, orioles, and cardinal grosbeaks flit among the green branches.

On the morning of Pony-penning Day the volunteer firemen turn into cowboys as they go out to round up the wild ponies. First the men go to Wallop's Island, where they divide into groups to hunt for the pony herds and strays. The men search carefully along the shore line, for they know the ponies like to take a dip in the surf to lessen the pain of horsefly stings.

The stallions kick, squeal, and bite as they are driven into waiting barges. The mares and colts are gentle and easier to handle. All the ponies are towed across the channel to Chincoteague, and driven into corrals.

The firemen often tell the story of "Little Black," the stallion who would not be caught. He was so fast and so clever that year after year he escaped. Once the men thought they had "Little Black" trapped on a high point of rock, but when they came within roping distance, the pony leaped into the surf and swam out to sea. Later he returned to land far down the coast — but by that time Pony-pen-

41

ning Day was over, and "Little Black" was safe for another year.

At low tide the ponies on Assateague Island are herded across the hundred-yard channel and into the pens at the carnival grounds.

Where do these wild ponies come from? Animal experts say they are not real ponies, but horses which have become stunted by their diet of marsh grass and salty water. Their ancestors were horses that were left on the islands in early colonial times.

Some say the Chincoteague ponies are descendants of Arabian horses left by pirates during the days of the Spanish Main. Or they may have swum ashore from a Spanish galleon wrecked off the Virginia coast.

Others say that Ponce de Leon brought horses with him on his search for the fountain of youth in Florida, and that they later wandered north.

Probably the true story is that the ponies, or stunted

42

horses, are descended from animals hidden on the islands by early colonial planters who wished to avoid paying taxes on them.

Everyone is merry and gay on Pony-penning Day. Hundreds of children and their parents crowd into the amusement grounds. They ride the merry-go-round, and look down on the island from high up in the Ferris wheel. They eat "snowballs" made of crushed ice and colored flavoring while they wait for the auction to begin.

"Now what am I bid for this handsome pony?" the loud voice of the auctioneer goes on. "Think of the years of happiness and pleasure he will bring your boy or girl!" He points his finger at a tall man, who nods his head. "I have a bid now of two hundred dollars! . . . Who will say two hundred and ten?"

Billy tugs at the tail of his striped polo shirt and begs again, "Please, Dad, bid! Bid on this one!"

Betty seizes her father's hand and says, "I think he's the most beautiful pony of all!"

Their father smiles, then nods his head at the auctioneer.

The auctioneer brings down his gavel with a loud thump. "Going . . . going . . . Sold! Sold to the father of the boy in the striped shirt!"

Billy's eyes light up with joy as he turns to his sister. "Do you know what I'd like to name our pony? Let's call him Chinco . . . for Chincoteague Island!"

Halloween

"Come on, Betty, it's time to get started," Bob calls to his sister. He is wearing a red devil costume with a long tail. Betty wears a black witch costume with a tall pointed hat.

"Just a minute. I have to help Mary Sue into her rabbit costume," Betty says.

Mary Sue is only three, but she wants to join in the fun. She is wearing a fluffy white costume with a white ball of fur at the back and two long, pink-lined ears.

Their mother hands each of them a brown paper bag, and the three children leave the house. Billy and Barbara, who live next door, join them. Billy wears a black costume painted with white to look like a skeleton. Barbara is dressed to look like a Dutch girl.

It is early evening, just after twilight. The night is crisp and clear, and there is a feeling of excitement in the air.

45

Other children come out of houses all round the block. They are dressed as ghosts and elves, fairies and farmers, ballerinas and "bums." Some carry jack-o-lanterns to light their way.

It is Halloween, October 31, and all over the United States children join in celebrating the occasion. Halloween is so named because it comes on the night before All Hallows or All Saints' Day, a religious feast. Long ago, people

46

thought that ghosts and witches could wander on earth this one night in the year. On this night, just for fun, children in the United States wear ghost, witch, and other costumes. They go from door to door asking for "handouts."

"We go just to the houses where there is a light on the porch," Betty explains to her little sister. "A light on the porch means that the people have something for us."

The masqueraders troop up the steps of a big white house, and Bob rings the bell. The door is opened by a friendly-looking lady with gray hair. She says, "Well, well! Look who is here! What do you want?"

"Handout, please." The children hold out their open paper bags, and the lady drops something into each one.

"Thank you! Thank you!" the children say. They do not look inside the bags until they are under the street lamp.

"What did she give us?" a ghost asks.

"Cinnamon apples! Good!"

The fallen leaves rustle under their feet as the children hurry from house to house all round the block. After a while the little rabbit says her legs are growing tired, and the witch says, "I think we have enough sweets now. Let's go home."

Back at home they empty the contents of their bags on the dining room table. There are oh's and ah's of delight as they see the apples and oranges, chewing gum and candy, cookies and gingerbread men. There are popcorn balls and candy kisses, wrapped in orange and black paper. There are bright-colored cream candies in Halloween shapes: witches, pumpkins, black cats, owls, and corn kernels.

Little Mary Sue is ready for bed, but Betty and Bob are going to a Halloween party given by a school friend who lives nearby. Still wearing their costumes, they walk to the house.

Two ghosts greet them at the door.

"Don't say a word," Betty whispers to Bob. "There will probably be a prize for the last person guessed, and your voice may give you away."

The rooms inside the house are almost dark. They are lighted only by the dim glow from jack-o'- lanterns placed high, in safe places. Dried corn stalks rustle in the corners, and paper skeletons hang in the doorways. A gypsy fortune teller sits in a booth, ready to tell fortunes with cards or by reading palms.

After the prizes for the costumes have been given out, the children take off their masks. The hostess shows them how to play Halloween games. Then they go to the kitchen to bob for apples placed in a tub of water on the floor. Betty thinks she will drown before she is finally able to catch an apple in her teeth without touching it with her hands.

Someone asks for ghost stories, and all the lights are turned out. The children shiver and shudder as the hostess tells the first story. Then the children take turns in telling scary tales.

There are Halloween things to eat. The children enjoy the pumpkin pie and doughnuts. The ice cream is orange in color, and the cookies have funny faces made with frosting. The guests have a choice of milk or fresh apple cider to drink.

"Halloween is always such fun!" Betty says when she

thanks her hostess for the nice party. "I wish it came more often."

"But we still have our handouts," Bob reminds her. "They'll last for a long, long time."

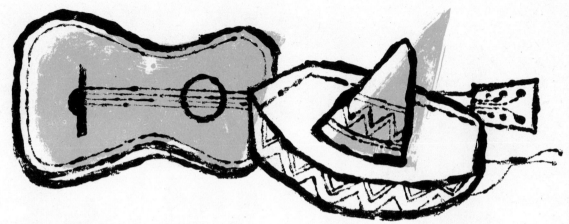

The Festival of Posadas

"Lupe, you may be the angel who guides the pilgrims," Mamacita Martinez says as she hands her small daughter a lighted candle.

Lupe's dark eyes glow with pride and pleasure at being singled out for such an honor.

"José and Manuel will carry the platform with the statues of Mary, Joseph, and the burro."

The two boys look very serious as they lift the platform to their shoulders and take their place in the procession.

"And the rest of the children will be the pilgrims. Here is a candle for you, Juanita, and one for you, Dolores."

Mamacita continues to hand lighted tapers to all the children in the neighborhood: Fidel and Luis, Miguel and Carlos, Pedro and Benito, Olivia, Elena, Margarita, and little Candelaria.

"Now . . . are we all ready to start?" she asks.

51

It is the evening of December 16, and all over the Republic of Mexico, in the cities and in the villages, processions like this are forming to celebrate the festival of Posadas, or the "lodgings." It recalls the journey of Mary and Joseph to Bethlehem, and lasts nine nights, ending on Christmas Eve.

Since the beginning of this festival is religious in spirit, the children are very serious as the procession moves slowly along the dark street. The candles cast flickering shad-

ows as the children walk along, chanting the Litany of the
Virgin.

"There is the first house. We're supposed to stop there,"
someone whispers.

Pedro, one of the larger boys, steps up, knocks on the
door, and sings in a sad tone,

"In the name of Heaven I beg for shelter.

Mary, my wife, can go no farther!"

From inside comes the angry reply,

53

"Begone, begone, this is no inn.

You may be thieves. I do not trust you.

There is no *posada,* no lodging here!"

The children shake their heads sadly and move on to the next place. Again and again they are turned away.

Finally they come to a house that is bright with lights. It is the Gonzalez home. Señor Gonzalez opens wide the door and joyfully bids them welcome.

"Enter, Mary, Queen of Heaven!

Welcome, Joseph, to this poor *puesto!*"

The children troop inside to find the house decorated for a party. The patio, or courtyard, is gay too, with lilies, Spanish moss, evergreens, and lighted lanterns.

First the visitors kneel at the tiny altar which has been prepared with a *nacimiento,* or nativity scene. But the tiny crib is empty. At the altar they all recite several Ave Marias and sing hymns which are special to the season.

When the religious ceremony is over, everyone is ready for fun. Wandering music-makers strum their guitars. Children and grownups dance in the patio, and food is served.

But the children can scarcely wait for the biggest moment: the breaking of the *piñata.* A *piñata* is made from a large clay jar, covered with colored tissue paper to look like a butterfly, a star, a fish, a burro, or perhaps an airplane or a sailing ship. The *piñata* at the Gonzalez home is a beautiful bird.

The clay jar is filled to the brim with candy, peanuts, tiny dolls and little toys, packages of chewing gum, oranges and apples, and other things that delight Mexican boys and girls. Sometimes there are *jicamas*, vegetables that look like turnips and taste oh, so crisp and juicy!

"Papacito," Margarita Gonzalez finally whispers to her father, "now it is time to break the *piñata*."

The children follow their host out to the patio. They watch him tie a rope to the *piñata*, then swing the rope over the branch of a tree. In this way he may raise and lower the *piñata* and trick the blindfolded children when they try to strike it.

"Let Candelaria try first because she is the smallest," someone shouts.

A handkerchief is folded and tied around the little girl's dark eyes and long black braids. She takes a stout stick, and the children whirl her around three times. Then she steps forward and swings at the jar with all her might.

But the *piñata*, the beautiful bird, flies upward and Candelaria misses it. The *piñata* is not broken.

The children jump up and down.

"Let me try! Let me try!"

All of them have a chance. José and Manuel, Juanita and Dolores, Fidel and Luis, Miguel and Carlos, Pedro and Benita, Olivia, Elena, and Margarita all try to break the *piñata*, but all of them fail.

At last only little Lupe Martinez is left. The children blindfold her, and Lupe takes the stick in her hands as Señor Gonzalez lowers the *piñata*.

"Now, Lupe, now!" the children shout.

Lupe gives the beautiful bird a ringing blow, and the *piñata* breaks. Candy, peanuts, toys, oranges, apples, all the lovely things in it rain to the floor, and the children scramble for them.

The evening is great fun. Each night of Posadas the children make a pilgrimage to a different home and enjoy breaking a *piñata*. But most of all they enjoy Christmas Eve, the final night of Posadas. At the last house, on that evening, they find the altar beautifully decorated with sparkling silver tinsel and flowers. And a tiny figure of the Christ Child lies in the little *pesebre*, or crib, which up to now has been empty. Or, in some places, the children, dressed as shepherds, stand silently by while the Christ Child is placed in the crib.

57

Late in the evening *tamales* are served. They are made of minced chicken and corn meal wrapped in corn husks. Then come *buñuelos*, pancakes dripping with honey, and a drink, *atole de chocolate.*

Before the guests leave for midnight Mass they gather round the *pesebre* to sing a lullaby to the Christ Child.

Lupe is tired but happy as she says, "*Buenas noches,* good night!" to everyone.

And everyone replies, "*Buenas noches,* and *Feliz Navidad!* Merry Christmas!"

Index

About the author

Alma Kehoe Reck is a former librarian who now combines two careers: advertising copywriter and author of books for children. Her interest in festivals began when she read of Turkey's Candy Festival in a travel book for adults; and it was further whetted when, soon after, she heard of the Befana Fair. Interviews with the natives of many lands followed, and from the wealth of colorful information she gathered, THE FIRST BOOK OF FESTIVALS took shape. Other books for children by Mrs. Reck include:

The Little Boy Lost
The West from A to Z
and
A Book of Holidays

The FIRST BOOKS